THE GRAND STRATEGIST

W9-AHL-473

To enable my people to achieve . . .

STRONGER STRATEGIC POSITIONS

My people know more about their business than I do. I help them not to fail by making sure they take account of the principles of competition:

DIRECTION

1 How clear and achievable are their goals?
2 Are they exploiting emerging trends quickly and effectively?

FOCUS

3 Do they have superior scale in the critical resource areas?
4 Are they using resources efficiently and with minimum waste?
5 Have they built enough flexibility of resources into their plans?

IMPLEMENTATION

6 Does the plan have the ability to gain key people's commitment?
7 How well are they creating barriers to competitive countermoves?
8 How unexpected and original is what they plan to do?
9 How simple are their plans to understand and implement?

HIGHER QUALITY IMPLEMENTATION

Selection, evaluation and training are my most powerful tools for fulfilling our mission. I will:
❏ inculcate and reward personal responsibility and individual initiative in every one of my people
❏ pay close attention to detail when it matters to my strategy, and not pick my people's plans to pieces when it doesn't
❏ learn from our mistakes and be objective in my evaluation of our experience
❏ allow no exceptions to our mission, and go to any lengths to be true to it

MORE EFFECTIVE RENEWAL

How I spend my time, what I reward . . . and punish, whom I promote and where I allocate our resources will determine the real climate of my organization. I will:
❏ conduct all our affairs in a spirit of play, and make sure it is possible for everyone else to do the same
❏ model and reinforce the ability to work in groups
❏ encourage constructive argument and help my people enjoy it
❏ remain open to criticism, and never shoot the bearers of bad news

. . . than our competitors

STR

MIKE DAVIDSON

THE GRAND ATEGIST

**THE
REVOLUTIONARY
NEW MANAGEMENT
SYSTEM**

**HENRY HOLT AND COMPANY
NEW YORK**

Henry Holt and Company, Inc.
Publishers since 1866
115 West 18th Street
New York, New York 10011

Henry Holt ® is a registered trademark
of Henry Holt and Company, Inc.

First published in the United States in 1995 by
Henry Holt and Company, Inc.
Originally published in the United Kingdom in 1995 by
Macmillan London Limited.

Library of Congress Cataloging-in-Publication Data
is available upon request.

ISBN 0-8050-4612-7

Henry Holt books are available for special promotions
and premiums. For details contact: Director, Special Markets.

First American Edition—1995

Printed in the United States of America
All first editions are printed on acid-free paper. ∞

10   9   8   7   6   5   4   3   2

FOREWORD:

THE AGE OF STRATEGIC MANAGEMENT

Every organization has competitors. Businesses compete to sell their products and services. Cities and states compete to attract new industries, contracts or government funds. Schools and universities compete for students and to attract and hold a talented faculty. Start-up ventures and small companies compete for scarce resources to ensure their very survival. For a whole generation after the Second World War, a healthy, growing economy left room for many competitors to prosper alongside each other. Then in one decade, the seventies, the advent of a global market, scarce resources, expensive money and the end to steady growth changed the rules of the game. Achieving the *absolute* goals of an organization now depends on *relative* success. The search for a competitive edge, and management of the entire corporation to achieve and sustain it, are the central operating tasks of our time.

Strategic management creates the competitive edge that makes winners. It harnesses all the potential of an organization to this end by causing every day-to-day operating decision to be made in a pre-eminently strategic manner. *Everything* is done with the intention of securing competitive advantage. Strategic management is therefore a task for the whole organization all the time, not the province of specialists or a once-yearly undertaking. It is a way of thinking, a guide to action and the determinant for the behaviour of every member of the organization. Its goal is the creation of a set of *distinctive* capabilities, that have *special* value to a *particular* part of the market-place. By doing so it positions the organization for the sustained, superior performance that is the mark of strategic success.

While recognition of the need to manage in this way is growing, it has seldom been put successfully into practice. The principal reason for this lack of success has been our belief that strategy should concentrate on improving the allocation of our *financial* resources.

We have become very good at it. But so has everyone else, leaving little opportunity for achieving a winning margin. But still some companies outperform others. They are the few who have remembered a more important set of resources – the *human* ones. Behaviour turns out not just to matter but to be the determining factor. It provides the margins of competitiveness which dictate who wins and who merely participates.

Above all else, strategic management brings about individual and group behaviour that results in competitive advantage. It is first and foremost the management of people, not money. Why have most of us missed it?

We have been pursuing the wrong goal – the making of

money, not the creation of wealth. The business schools, so long the scapegoat, are a symptom not the cause. Society has put the rapid accumulation of personal riches at the pinnacle of success. The business schools, as good market-oriented institutions, have filled the need. The result has been too many manipulators of money and too few managers of people.

Lack of competitiveness cannot be blamed on the failure of educational institutions, loss of work ethic or a superior Japanese system. It is the result of narrow vision and the failure to lead.

To quote Thomas Watson, Jr, '. . . the real difference between success and failure in a corporation can very often be traced to the question of how well the organization brings out the great energies and talents of its people.'

That insight was the mark of a tiny number of outstanding companies when it was written in the mid-sixties. In an era marked by unprecedented competitive intensity and accelerating change, it has become a condition for survival. Today a whole new breed of leaders is managing by identifying the shared values that can create common cause, and developing the shared vision that can inspire the winning effort. In so doing they are at last ushering in The Age of Strategic Management.

This book is dedicated to that new breed of leader – The Grand Strategist.

Mike Davidson

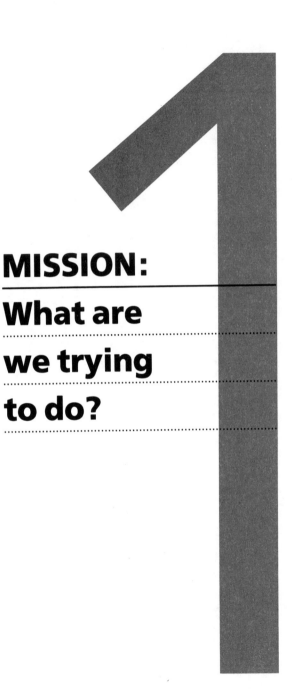

MISSION:

What are
we trying
to do?

1 HELP!

Once there was a very successful Manager.

He ran a big division of a large company and was very well paid for his success. He knew he had a shot at the President's job when she retired. But he wasn't happy. Each year it seemed he worked longer hours, and took shorter holidays. Each new promotion somehow resulted in less satisfaction not more. Life seemed to be one long struggle with unanticipated crises. Each success came harder than the last, and each failure was more difficult to correct. It wasn't that there were failures that bothered him, but that he didn't really understand why they happened. On reflection, he didn't really understand the reasons for the successes either. He seemed to be doing the same things but sometimes they worked, and sometimes they didn't.

It hadn't always been thus.

He could remember the time early in his career when things seemed to go right almost all of the time. And when they went wrong he immediately knew why and could learn from the failure to do even better next time.

He smiled to himself in memory because no one had expected him to do so well.

He had been an average student, at a moderately good school.

However, he had obviously done something right, though he never learned what, in the eyes of the big company's campus recruiter. He took to business like a duck to water. He worked hard because he enjoyed it, so he became known as a self-starter. His cheerfulness made him popular with his peers. The company's customers found his enthusiasm and energy infectious. Gradually people came to call on him to handle the difficult tasks. He could be relied upon to keep cool in a crisis.

He moved quickly through the ranks and before long he was promoted to manager.

Again he took to it as if it was second nature. He was good at motivating people. Praising and reprimanding came easily to him. Because he understood his subordinates' tasks so well he was good at setting objectives and allocating the right amount of resources to achieve them.

Most of the time the results were just what he hoped, and he began to get the reputation of someone who got the job done. When, occasionally, it didn't work out as expected he did find himself wondering whether he could have done better, and whether there was a *system* that he could follow which would help him be even more successful. But he was doing well, and didn't have enough time to worry much about anything except the challenge immediately before him.

In any case his superiors were delighted. He got things done, he didn't need much supervision and people liked to work for him. Better still he didn't play games with his budgets, or in his financial reporting, so they could rely on what he said his group could do. Top management began to notice his successes.

When the job of running a small division became unexpectedly vacant it was decided to give him a shot.

He was ecstatic. He was the youngest general manager in the company's history since the founder. Nobody was jealous because it was felt that he had earned the right. Now he would see what he could do with a whole business.

Shortly after he took over, a new product bombed. He was in his element, soothing customers, adjusting budgets, reassigning people, putting on a full court press to make up for the lost sales. He didn't have time to reflect on why the product had failed. Anyway it had been generated under his predecessor's leadership so it didn't reflect on him. Six months later he approved a plan to develop a new market and watched one of his rising young sales managers turn it into a great success. But shortly thereafter another, as far as he could tell similar, venture with just as good a champion didn't work out at all.

Again he picked up the pieces superbly and had his

division back on track with hardly a blip in its performance. But this time it seemed to take more out of him than the time before. 'Moreover,' he said to himself, 'surely I should have been able to avoid the problem in the first place.' The nagging concern that he was missing something began to return more and more often to his thoughts.

And so it went. Some successes, some failures, and some in-between. On balance he was still outperforming his peers so top management was well pleased. And before long came the next promotion.

And not long after that the next.

But each time it was becoming more of a struggle. And he was getting further and further removed from where the action was. He had to rely more and more on secondhand information, and others to implement his ideas. Worst of all there were now too many crises occurring within his span of responsibilities for him to deal with all of them himself. He fretted. He fumed. And finally he decided there must be a better way.

So he began to ask other managers what he could do better. Half of them didn't have the time to answer him. And the other half thought *he* should be giving *them* the answers.

He started to look at business books and magazines more carefully to see if they had anything to offer. A lot of them suggested the answer was something called 'strategic management'. Many of them seemed to contain some interesting ideas about planning, but none of them gave him a system he could use to guide him and his people through their everyday, operating challenges.

Then one day, at a cocktail party, a friend told him about the Chief Executive of a large group of companies, who, it was claimed, had found the secret of success. His companies consistently outperformed their competition under all conditions. His people weren't suffering from the same frustrations that the manager and his friend were feeling. They succeeded more often in what they tried, failed less, and, his friend said, seemed to understand why. This amazing person was known as the Grand Strategist. Somebody with such a fancy name won't have time for me, thought the manager. But every so often he thought about the strange name, and wondered what it meant.

Then suddenly the President of his company decided to retire early. The Chairman called him in and told him the Board wanted him as the new CEO. Of course he accepted. But inwardly he was in a state of near panic. I can only just cope with my current job, he thought. What do I do now that I have it all? How do I help all my old peers do their jobs, now that they report to me? And, what is my answer to the new manager who asks me for a system to manage by? Then he remembered the story of the Grand Strategist. So, in desperation, he gave him a call.

2 THE GRAND STRATEGIST

The Grand Strategist sounded pleased to hear from him, and eager to help. 'Come over tomorrow,' he said, 'and for as long as you like.'

The next day the new President arrived at the Grand Strategist's offices, which were elegant, but not nearly as large or as opulent as he had expected for such a successful and powerful person. When the secretary showed him in he had another surprise. There were no papers on the Grand Strategist's desk! Just a pad of paper, a pencil and a little plaque with some writing on it which he couldn't see.

'Now, how can I help?' asked the Grand Strategist.

'Well,' said the new President, 'I've just about come to the end of my tether. I don't know anyone who is better at running an operation than I am. But I seem to spend most of my time cleaning up messes; and the rest of it reviewing proposals from people who know more about their business than I do. Now they have made me the President of the company. Right now my only idea is to do what I have been doing, only better. And somehow . . . '

'. . . it ought to be a different kind of job,' finished the Grand Strategist.

'Yes, how did you guess?' said the new President.

'Well, you're not the first, you know,' said his host. 'But you have already taken the first two steps.'

'The first *two*?' said the new President. 'I guess the first was recognizing I must be missing something. But the second? Oh, you mean seeking advice.'

'That's right,' said the Grand Strategist. 'But you'd be surprised how few managers have taken *either* step. Now, where shall we begin?'

'Perhaps,' said the new President, 'you could explain how someone who runs such a large, complex business doesn't have any papers on his desk, and could spare me an unlimited amount of time at such short notice.'

'Oh, I don't run the company,' said the Grand Strategist. 'Everybody else does that. I manage the Mission.'

The new President was very confused, and showed it in his expression. But before he could ask for some clarification, the Grand Strategist turned on a television that was standing in the corner of the room. Some beautiful violin music began to play and then a whole series of quotations appeared on the screen one by one.

The ultimate goal of the corporation is survival.

Peter Drucker

In order to be saved you must know what you believe,
know why you believe it, and know how to act upon it.

St Thomas Aquinas

To accomplish great things we must not only act but also
dream, not only plan but also believe.

Anatole France

Man does not live by bread alone, but by faith, by
admiration, by sympathy.

Ralph Waldo Emerson

Even bad doctrine is better than none at all. You can test
it, differ from it, your mind has something to bite on. You
need the rock to plant the lighthouse.

Joyce Cary

Strong beliefs win strong men and make them stronger.

Walter Bagehot

I ought, therefore I can.

Immanuel Kant

Order is not a pressure which is imposed on society from
without, but an equilibrium that is set up from within.

Jose Ortega Gasset

A society cannot exist without rules.

Charles Smith

Virtue naturally procures considerable advantages to the virtuous.

Joseph Butler

Strong convictions precede great actions. The man strongly possessed by an idea is the master of all who are uncertain or wavering. Clear, deeply held convictions rule the world.

James Freeman Clark

The secret of success is constancy to purpose.

Benjamin Disraeli

The happiest excitement in life is to be convinced that one is fighting for all one is worth on behalf of some clearly seen and deeply felt good and against some greatly scorned evil.

Ruth Benedict Arnold

Certainty and uniformity are gains not lightly to be sacrificed. Above all is this true where honest men have shaped their conduct on the faith of the pronouncement.

Justice Benjamin Cardozo

The desire of this age is for a doctrine which may serve to condense our knowledge, guide our researches and shape our lives, so that conduct may really be the consequence of belief.

George Henry Lewes

I firmly believe that any organization in order to survive and achieve success, must have a sound set of beliefs on which it premises all its policies and actions.

Next I believe that the most important single factor in corporate success is faithful adherence to those beliefs.

And finally, I believe if an organization is to meet the challenge of a changing world, it must be prepared to change everything about itself except those beliefs as it moves through corporate life.

Thomas Watson, Jr

'How do you feel now?' asked the Grand Strategist as he put up the lights again. 'Notice any difference?'

'Well, yes,' began the new President. 'Come to think of it, I do. I'm more relaxed. And I guess I'm intrigued. Did Thomas Watson really mean that, do you think? When did he write it?'

'As a matter of fact, he not only meant it, he wrote it, in 1963, in a book called *A Business and its Beliefs*, about the principles that he and his father used to build IBM,' said his host. 'There were three of them:

- Respect for the individual
- Major attention to service
- Superiority in all things.

'When IBM was at its best that book was the first thing every new manager in IBM was given to study; and the first topic at every new manager's training course was the meaning of those beliefs.'

'So the beliefs come first?' asked the new President.

'Yes,' said the Grand Strategist. 'And everyone must share them. You'll probably find that Shared Values is the best way to think of them. What do you think is their primary function?'

'To make sure everyone is on the same team?' tried the new President. 'To minimize internal conflict?'

'That's part of it,' said the Grand Strategist, 'but there is another, even more important reason. They provide a control system.' Again the new President looked confused. But then the Grand Strategist handed him a card on which was written:

Shared Values provide **CONTROL** by guiding behaviour.

'Have you ever thought how the Roman Catholic Church controls the largest, most international organization in the world with so few hierarchical levels?' asked the Grand

Strategist. 'The Church calls it Doctrine: a body of rules stemming from a common set of beliefs – or Shared Values. On which the Pope spends the major part of his time, right?'

'You mean, when people share the same set of values, the way they will react to a given situation can be relied upon to be the same?' began the new President hesitantly, and then, speeding up, 'And, by strengthening the depth with which they hold those values you strengthen the control system?'

'That's it,' said the Grand Strategist. 'And there's another wonderful advantage. This is the only control system in the world that doesn't depend on fear to operate!' Then seeing his guest looking puzzled, he continued, 'Every control system I'd ever seen anywhere in the world, until I was introduced to this one, depends on fear to work. If you don't follow this procedure, you'll be in trouble. If you break that rule you'll be punished. Controllers' manuals are full of rules and procedures that *must* be followed. What makes them work is the implication that some form of unpleasant consequence will be the result of ignoring them. Laws work the same way. They keep us behaving within certain boundaries for fear of the consequences if we step outside them. Now this kind of control system has two unfortunate side-effects. First it absorbs a huge amount of energy in police work to make it succeed. Second, what are the characteristics of people motivated by fear?'

'Avoidance of risk-tasking? Doing just enough to get by?' tried the new President.

'Right. Hardly what we need to get the creativity and extra effort we need to build a winning team,' said the Grand Strategist. 'In contrast how do people behave when they're engaged in something they fervently believe in?'

'Full of enthusiasm and new ideas. Put in long hours. Passionate in sticking to their beliefs,' said the new President. 'If anything you need a system to stop them going overboard, not the other way around!'

'Now *that's* the kind of control I don't mind engaging in,' said the Grand Strategist. 'In fact I spend a lot of my time doing just that: keeping my people's enthusiasm sensibly focused by our values, but doing so ever so tenderly, of course, so as not to damage their commitment.'

'I can certainly see the power in that idea,' said the new President. 'but what happens when someone does behave in a way that is inconsistent with your values?'

'That we can't, and don't tolerate,' said the Grand Strategist. 'Of course, mistakes and learning we expect and help with, but if someone can't eventually buy-in to our values sufficiently to act on them voluntarily, then we have to part company. Incidentally, that doesn't have to mean that he or she is a "bad" person. Our values and our way of implementing them are not for everyone, and we respect that. But our "control system" won't work if we tolerate exceptions.'

'That certainly puts some teeth into it. "Shared values provide control by guiding behaviour." It's a wonderful thought,' said the new President, 'but you said you managed your Mission not your Values, so I assume there's more to it.'

'Yes,' said the Grand Strategist. 'Remember the quote from Joyce Cary you just saw? It ended with, "You need the rock to plant the lighthouse." Shared Values provide the rock, but we also need the lighthouse to tell us the right direction to go in.' And he handed the new President a second card.

Shared Purposes provide **FOCUS** by driving strategy.

'The second part of my job is to help the organization determine what its purposes are and then make sure that they, like our values, are understood and shared by everyone.'

'What do you mean by purposes?' asked the new President. 'And how do you determine them?'

'Are you familiar with the term *stakeholders*?' began the Grand Strategist. 'No? Let me explain. Stakeholders are all the groups of people who have a stake in, or can have a major impact on, the performance of an organization. A typical list for a company might include Customers, Stockholders, Employees, Communities, Suppliers, the Public. For the company to survive and prosper over the long haul, it must have a mutually beneficial relationship with each of these groups. For it to outperform its competition, of course, it must offer something special to each of them. Those special "somethings" are its purposes.'

'So, after I've decided what the core values are for my

company I must work out what purposes it serves for each of the groups of people or institutions with which it interacts?' said the new President.

'That's right,' said the Grand Strategist. 'The two key questions are, "Who are my key stakeholders?" and "What need of theirs am I seeking to satisfy better than any of my competitors?" '

'Could you give me an example?' asked the new President.

'Certainly,' replied the Grand Strategist. 'Let's use a bit of modern folklore. I mentioned IBM's Beliefs, or Shared Values earlier. Let's consider what their purposes might have been, let's say in the seventies, when they were beating the world. How do you think we might describe their customers?'

'Everyone!' said his guest. 'First it was large organizations. Then they moved down to smaller ones. By the seventies it was just about anyone who used information-processing equipment.'

'Yes, exactly. Let's call them Information Equipment Users. And I think you'd agree that the one thing IBM was famous for was Service. What they were clearly seeking to offer their customers better than anyone else in the world was Service. Not Price. Or Speed. Or Power. Or the latest gizmo. Service. At a time when computers weren't very well understood, or very reliable, that proved to be more important to their customers than anything else. Now, what about another stakeholder group, their employees?'

'Well,' said the new President, 'I've known a lot of past and present employees of IBM and the best word I can think of to describe the relationship back then is "membership." Once they were accepted, which, assuming they were competent, I guess was determined by their buying into the shared values, they had a career for as long as they wanted it. In fact, I believe IBM said at that time that it had *never* laid anyone off due to market changes.'

'Membership sounds like a good word to me,' said the Grand Strategist, 'and I'd say that something like "creative, intelligent, career seekers" might describe the particular group of potential employees to whom IBM was trying to appeal. They clearly needed creativity and intelligence for the kind of business they were in. And IBM's practice of internal promotion, plus the importance they attached to their Beliefs and the amount they spent on training, certainly says they wanted their people to make their careers with them. Let me complete the list for you:

Stakeholders	Needs
Information Equipment Users	Service
Creative, Intelligent, Career-Seekers	Membership
Suppliers of Relevant Components	Secure Market
Software Writers	Partnership
The American People	Technological Security
Investors Seeking Capital Appreciation	Superior Returns

'The third group were the Suppliers of IBM-product components, for whom IBM provided a secure market. Notice how IBM's purposes for both suppliers and employees differ fundamentally from the way the major automobile companies treated those two stakeholder groups throughout most of their history. Under the pressure of Japanese competition, the major auto companies have finally been forced to move towards an IBM-like relationship with both their suppliers and employees, in search of the quality and productivity they need to survive. Changes at the level of Mission were the necessary precondition to making their new strategies of productivity and quality possible.

'A fourth key group is made up of Software Writers. Many years ago, it was common knowledge in the industry that IBM regarded independent software writers as the enemy. IBM sought to maintain close control of all the software written for its computers. The advent of mini- and then micro-computers, however, meant that the availability of extensive, creative software would determine the winner of the hardware contest. So IBM began to offer a "partnership" relationship to software writers, and thus provided them with tremendous opportunity while strengthening its own market position.

'The American People was another of IBM's stakeholder groups. IBM was quick to make the case for itself as one of the key guardians of the nation's technological security. It might not even be too far fetched to claim that its success in this effort was one of the major reasons why IBM and AT&T had very different outcomes in their confrontations with the Justice Department.

'Finally, IBM's stock did not pay a very big dividend. Investors seeking capital appreciation – not current income – were, in those happier days, its subset of the equity market, and it sought to offer them superior returns.'

'That's fascinating,' said the new President. 'I remember reading that in the mid-eighties IBM was the most valuable company on the New York Stock Exchange, and that, according to a survey at that time, it was also the most admired company in America. That list together with the Beliefs you mentioned earlier begins to suggest why.' He paused, then asked, 'Why have you put investors last? I guess I've always thought of creating wealth for its shareholders as a company's primary purpose.'

'That's easy,' said the Grand Strategist. 'To make a point. If we do all the other things successfully, we don't need to worry about the shareholders; they'll do fine!

'Actually,' he went on, 'it is a bit more complicated than that. The most important thing to recognize in listing out your purposes is that their achievements are interdependent. In other words the better-return-for-the-shareholder purpose follows from success at doing what the other stakeholders want. And, equally, in the long run, if you're not successful at eating an acceptable amount of wealth for your shareholders, you won't be around to try to satisfy the other groups! Consequently we have to join them together in our thinking. What we're really talking about here is how we're going to outperform others in relating to customers, employees, suppliers, etc, *so as to* achieve our economic aim of making more money for our shareholders.'

'I also noticed,' said the President, 'that you described how IBM's attitude to independent software writers had changed over the years. So Shared Purposes, unlike Shared Values, can vary over time?'

'Yes, in fact they must, as the environment changes,' said the Grand Strategist. 'What's more, in a large, complex company like mine they vary from division to division, and from department to department.'

'And that's OK,' said the new President, grasping the idea, 'because the Shared Values provide a common link, and secure foundation, even while everything else is different or changing.'

There was a pause. Then the new President had another thought. 'What went wrong?' he said. 'I mean, we just talked about IBM as it was in the seventies and early eighties. But look at it in the nineties. Stock price way down. New CEO from the outside. People leaving in what look to me like lay-offs. Doesn't that destroy the whole idea?'

'Well of course the whole story's not written yet,' said

the Grand Strategist, 'but I think we can make a good guess at some of the root causes. And I think you'll find they reinforce what we just talked about, not destroy it.

'Supposing IBM started to slip on service, or it became less important,' he said. 'What do you think would happen then?'

The new President thought for a moment.

'If they weren't better than anyone else on service or it mattered less,' he began, as he gathered his thoughts, 'then, a higher price would begin to hurt,' he continued, 'and lower speed, less power and not being state-of-the-art on product would kill them,' he finished in a rush.

'And what about their other values?' asked the Grand Strategist, 'what about "respect for the individual", and "superiority in everything we do"?'

'Well, I had heard that it was virtually impossible to fire anybody at IBM in the eighties, even if it was for good cause,' said the new President. 'In fact one IBMer told me he'd tried and it was so futile, despite the clear justification, that he'd decided never to bother to try again.'

'Right,' said the Grand Strategist, 'the original idea somehow got perverted into the right to a job for life under just about any circumstances.

'And something similar happened to the third value. It too got perverted from what I think was originally a very humble idea of seeking to excel at everything they undertook, to a "going first class, only the best is good enough" attitude which put their costs through the roof.'

'So it was hubris, and a failure to adapt the original ideas to changed circumstances,' said the new President. 'That makes sense and, as you said, it really does reinforce the basic concept, not refute it.

'But it sure says it's a bit more complex than it first sounded. You'd better keep your eyes open for success going to your head. And you'd better make sure everyone understands what you really mean all the time.'

'You're so right,' said the Grand Strategist, 'that's why it's a full-time job. Managing our Mission, I mean.'

3 THE MAGIC OF MISSION

The new President started again, 'I have a feeling it's not quite as easy to do it for your own organization as it seemed when we were going through that. And the stakes are awfully high if this really is to be the organization's driving force. I mean, if you get it wrong, or if nobody buys in, you're lost before you start.'

'You're quite right,' said the Grand Strategist. 'In fact, you may be worse off, because your credibility will be badly damaged if you aim at something that is clearly not reasonable, or declare a set of values which just don't fit the reality of your organization.

'And given that,' he went on, 'it is nothing short of tragic how little effort most organizations' leaders spend on their Missions – either formulating them properly, or managing them in their organizations. Of course, the result is that they can't delegate very well. Their various business and functional units define their own strategy according to their own agendas, and top management has to spend an inordinate amount of time acting as referee. Think how much more productive everyone can be when there is a common cause dominating all those parochial concerns. In fact I find that, by managing our Mission, I make a magical thing happen – people do the right things of their own accord!

'Mind you,' he went on, 'you have to remember as I said a little while ago, that it is a full-time job, and that even I need reminding. Which is why I keep this on my desk, and look at it whenever I'm faced with a decision.'

And he turned round the plaque that his visitor had noticed when he came in.

> If I manage our Mission I can rely on everyone else to run the business.
>
> Before I take any decision I ask myself:
>
> 'In what way will this action embody our Values?'
> 'In what way will this action contribute to our Purposes?'

The new President was silent. He knew he had made a huge step towards understanding his new job. He had much to think about. He was beginning to realize what had been the source of his rising discontent as a manager all these years. If only he had learned all this when he'd been given his *first* managerial assignment, not after he'd just accepted his last! Everyone needed his new understanding – it was the key to every manager's job, not just the President's. Moreover, he thought to himself, I need to use this thinking on myself not just my company if I really want it to work.

The Grand Strategist broke into his reverie. 'I think, from your silence, that we've gone far enough for today,' he said. 'It's been a pleasure talking to you. Call me if I can be of any more help.' And he wished his visitor farewell.

The new President spent much of the next few days thinking about what he'd learned. In the following weeks, as he began to use this new way of approaching his job, he made a list of the actions that made the ideas work most powerfully for him:

1   Constantly use words and phrases from our Mission whenever I speak or write to my people.

2   Devote all the time anyone wants to explain our Mission, all its components, and their vital relevance to everything we do.

3   Show people the connection between our Values and Purposes, and the business decisions I make – particularly when I say 'no'.

4   Encourage people to challenge decisions, rules and activities they see as inconsistent with our Values and Purposes.

5   Get my people to rate me on how they perceive me living up to our Values.

6   Use our Values as the basis for promotion decisions, and performance evaluations of my people – and make sure people know I am.

7   Share a quantified score card of what it means to achieve our Purposes with my people.

8   Celebrate actions which, and people who, personify particular aspects of our Values.

9   Reflect our Values and Purposes in all my organization's communications.

10   Refer to our Mission in my external dealings, in particular with customers, suppliers and potential recruits.

He also made a brief summary of what he'd learned from the Grand Strategist to keep in front of himself all the time.

THE GRAND STRATEGIST'S CREDO

MISSION

Shared Values provide **CONTROL** by guiding behaviour.

Shared Purposes provide **FOCUS** by driving strategy.

If I manage our Mission I can rely on everyone else to run the business.

Before I take any decision I ask myself:

'In what way does this action embody our Values?
'In what way does this action contribute to our Purposes?'

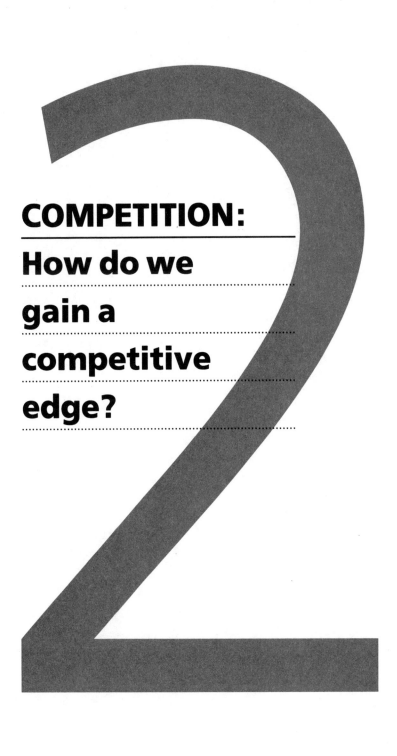

COMPETITION:

How do we gain a competitive edge?

1 THE AIM OF STRATEGY

The new President found that reflecting on Values and Purposes was a lonely job. So he brought some close colleagues together into a group to explore them with him. They found that, by tracing the reasons for their company's success back to the special beliefs that had guided their founders, they could quite easily agree on the core values that they felt distinguished it.

But when they tested their ideas on their colleagues they discovered that they needed a much broader involvement of people than just the top team to create a true credo that everyone would use to guide their behaviour.

People throughout the organization cared deeply about the subject. They weren't about to accept a set of values imposed on them from above. They had an intuitive grasp of the importance of values belonging *voluntarily* to everyone, as they had when the company had been in its early, formative days. Moreover it became clear that the leaders were going to have to hold themselves to a very high standard of conduct if they were serious about this new way of running the company.

Others would follow the lead they gave by observing what they practised, not what they preached.

Somewhat chastened, and a lot more cautiously, the new President and his colleagues turned to the issue of Purposes. Defining broad groups of stakeholders was not a difficult task. But then they got stuck. The new President called the Grand Strategist again.

'We've determined what our Values are,' he said, 'and we're already seeing a difference in attitude from our people in response to our new care in staying faithful to them; a little bit of the magic you mentioned, maybe. I think we also know who are our stakeholders, and what, broadly, we're trying to do for them. But we're having a lot of trouble wrestling with the "better than anyone else" bit.'

'That was a difficult step for me, too,' said the Grand Strategist. 'And I still need help there. But I have a friend who is a real expert, so why don't you talk to him.'

A couple of days later the man found himself entering a tiny, very untidy office to talk to a harassed-looking consultant.

'Come in. Delighted to see you. The Grand Strategist said you needed help figuring out what you can do better than your competition,' said the Consultant.

'Yes,' said the new President. 'And, as a matter of fact, more than that. I guess I haven't fully grasped why I'm trying to figure it out.'

'Let's back up a bit,' said the Consultant. 'I assume one

of your purposes is to create superior wealth for your shareholders, right?' The new President nodded. 'Good, now how do you do that?'

'By making higher returns and growing faster than our competition,' said the new President.

'What about risk?'

'Well, I suppose I was assuming a comparable level of risk,' said the new President. 'But I guess, now that I think about it, another way would be to make the same return with lower risk.'

'Right,' said the Consultant. 'The key factors are return, and the reliability or security of that return. We'll deal with growth in a minute. You are trying to outperform comparable investments your shareholders could make on those two factors. Now, how you do that is to outperform competition in your business. There are two elements of that competition – strategy and tactics. The latter is how all of your operating people deal with the day-to-day interaction with competition in the market-place. Your job, as their leader, is to deal with the former: strategy. So let me give you a definition of strategy to move us along:

> The aim of Strategy is to achieve positions of sustained advantage which result in:

- Higher returns
- More secure returns than comparable investments.

'Remember, your concern is not with the actual, day-to-day competition in the market-place. Your operating managers are there to take care of that. Your job is to load the odds in their favour before any competition ever takes place, i.e., to give them superior *positions* from which to compete. In fact the supreme, strategic accomplishment is to have your competitor believe your position is so strong he concedes without a fight.'

'I think I understand what you're getting at,' said the new President, 'but an illustration would help.'

'Of course,' said the Consultant. 'It's not an intuitively obvious idea. Our experience, for example in the stock market, leads us to expect higher returns to be accompanied by higher risks, and more secure investments to yield lower returns. So it's quite a challenge to say that the aim of strategy is to beat this expectation. In fact, there is a simple, graphical way to show that this is truly accomplishable.

'Imagine two competitors making an interchangeable product so selling it for the same price. If one competitor has lower costs than the other he will clearly enjoy higher returns – the first goal of strategy. Let's say 15 per cent on sales, compared to 10 per cent as this shows,' and he handed the new President a card:

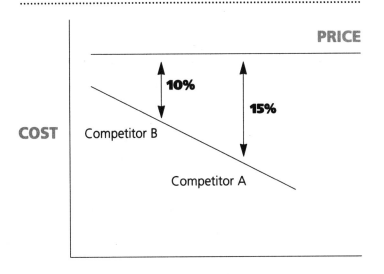

'As you can see Competitor A has a higher return than the Competitor B when both of them get the same price, because of the difference in their costs.

'Now think what happens in a recession, or a downturn in the requirement for the particular product. For a time supply exceeds demand which makes everyone compete a bit harder, and forces down the price by, say, 5 per cent. The result is a 50 per cent reduction in Competitor B's margin (from 10 to 5 per cent), but only 33 per cent in Competitor A's (from 15 to 10 per cent) because of its lower costs. That means Competitor A is achieving a higher, *and* more secure (in the sense that it is less affected by bad times) return, at one and the same time.

'From this little example we consultants used to draw the conclusion that strategy must focus on relative cost. That the aim of strategy could and would be gained by achieving and sustaining a superior, relative cost position to competition. The vast bulk of the strategy development work done in the seventies stemmed from that idea. Achieving and exploiting a sustainable cost advantage became the core idea on which most business strategy during that decade was developed.'

'So the "position of advantage" you talked about is the lower relative cost?' asked the President. 'And obviously you need to sustain it if your success is to continue.'

'That's right,' said the Consultant, 'but we soon learned that lower cost, or superior efficiency, by itself, isn't enough. Nor in fact is it the only kind of position that will achieve the aim of higher and more secure returns. I imposed the condition of an interchangeable product, hence equal price on the two competitors in my example. If one of them can sufficiently differentiate its product it can achieve higher price realization and, from that source, the same strategic result. IBM for a long time did that with Service. McDonald's does it with Quality, and Rolls-Royce with Status are other examples. In fact, differentiation for many companies is today a much more likely source of success than efficiency. As their industries have matured, and information has become widely shared within them, many competitors have been able to achieve pretty similar levels of efficiency.

'Of course this does not mean that efficiency no longer matters. Quite the contrary, achieving a competitive level of efficiency is the condition for starting the race at all. The condition for winning it, though, has become, in most industries, differentiation, and yet more differentiation, in shorter and shorter cycles as everyone tries to get ahead.'

'I certainly understand the concept,' said the new President. 'Now how do you apply it?'

'Good question,' said the Consultant. 'Let's explore it with another example.'

2 THE SECRET OF SUCCESS

'Scandinavian Airlines, some years ago, determined that its primary purpose was to be the airline for the business traveller. It chose from all the possible sets of customers, business people as the particular part of the market-place on which to focus. And of course, it knew what it wanted to do for them better than anyone else: be their supplier of rapid, long distance, mostly international transport, from a base in northern Europe.'

'So that statement of purpose defined the scope of their business in the sense of what services, and what market?' asked the new President.

'Yes. Now the next issue they faced was how to achieve their purpose. So they asked themselves, "What distinctive capabilities could we develop that business people, in particular, value in an airline, so that they'll choose us before other airlines and may even be prepared to pay extra for it?" One of the answers was – to run our planes on time. Being on time is something that the business traveller puts a high value on. To satisfy that need better than other airlines would translate – along with a lot of other things – into achievement of our purpose; and SAS believed it could do that. The point is you can't just choose a purpose, i.e., a set of products and a set of markets, in a vacuum. You have to know how to achieve it, and of course, you have to test that it is feasible with your resources.'

'So the choice of purposes, and the development of strategies to achieve them, is an iterative process to end up with something which is both acceptable and achievable?' asked the new President.

'Right,' said the Consultant. 'The key step is to identify the distinctive set of capabilities which appeal to your targeted segment of the market-place, and then test whether you can achieve leadership at them, relative to your competitors. If you can, strategic success, i.e., higher and more secure returns, will follow.'

The new President wrote down what he had learned:

STRATEGY: PLAN IT

Success is the reward for excelling at a set of **distinctive capabilities** that have **special** value to a **particular** part of the market-place.

'That deals with superior profitability, now how about growth?' he asked.

'I'm glad you came back to that,' said the Consultant, 'because more money has been squandered by ill-advised attempts to grow than any other consciously adopted kind of plan I have ever seen.'

'Many companies jumped on to the bandwagon of relative cost-based strategies by making market-share their primary strategic objective, so as to improve their scale relative to their competitors. Very few weighed the cost of the share-gaining strategies against the benefits that would accrue. Price wars erupted all over the place. Over-capacity became chronic in industry after industry. The growth often ended up by hurting profitability rather than enhancing it. So what *is* the source of desirable, or profitable growth?

'Basically it is matching distinctive capabilities with emerging trends. "Win with the winner" in the oldest and truest of all the marketing maxims, referring to the idea that, if you can make the winning companies in your customer industries your customers, then you will outgrow your competitors as they outgrow theirs. The difficulty of course is that once these companies are known all your competitors will be trying to do the same thing. So the strategic secret is to catch them when they are only just emerging, and to develop great superiority in the capabilities that they value before anyone else can. Every explosive success you'll observe will stem from someone achieving this match – from Apple and software for people who really wanted to use computers as word processors, to Federal Express and overnight mail, and even Peters and Waterman with *In Search of Excellence* for an emerging market for business books on how to manage people.'

The new President added to his summary:

> Profitable growth comes from exploiting our strengths, while avoiding our competitors', to satisfy emerging needs.

He looked up. 'Is there anything to help us test our ideas short of actually trying them out?' he asked.

'Well of course you can never be certain,' said the Consultant. 'But there is a set of principles against which we can test our ideas. In fact they can do more than that: they can help us add strategy to the way our people run their operations. Let me explain.'

3 ADDING STRATEGY TO OPERATIONS

'"War is nothing but a duel on an extensive scale", wrote Clausewitz, one of the greatest thinkers on strategy ever,' the Consultant began. 'So let's start there, with that most basic form of conflict to derive some principles for testing our strategic ideas.

'A duellist, let us say a boxer, has to do four things – to think, to guard, to move and to hit. Before fighting each fighter must *think* through his plan for how he is going to beat his adversary. What is his objective, i.e., how is he going to win? Knock his opponent out? Disable him? Win on points? Then, during the actual experience of putting it into practice, he must be able to alter his tactics, and maybe even his objective. For, as General Patton once said, "No plan ever survives contact with the enemy!" Next he must be able to *guard* against his opponent's offence. Third he must be able to *move* into a position where he can take the offensive, so that, finally, he can *hit* his opponent and knock him out.

'From these four basic elements of what goes on in a fight we can derive four, corresponding principles: The principles of

The Objective, of Security, of Mobility and of The Offensive.

'Staying with our boxer, as he develops the skills that come from experience, he will soon recognize three further keys to his success. He will seek to economize his strength so as not to exhaust himself prematurely; he will try to use his weight to apply superior strength, e.g., leaning on his opponent or hitting him harder than he himself is hit; and he will attempt to surprise him, that is, catch him off guard by doing something he is not expecting.

'So we arrive at three more principles: of Economy, of Mass and of Surprise.

'Now, when we take this rather basic form of competition up a level of complexity, so that it now involves two *groups* of fighters, we find that, to achieve the aims of the first seven principles, we have to add two more. We need to ensure that all the members of our force understand the objective, and that all their actions are co-ordinated towards it. And, finally we will find that the more people involved, the more propensity there will be for confusion, misunderstanding and misinterpretation of orders. We will need to keep things as simple as possible.

'So we come to the last two principles: Unity of Command, and Simplicity.

'These are known as the nine Principles of War. Making them useful in the context of business strategy requires a couple of small adjustments.

'First, business is not, in general, about discrete "campaigns" and "battles", but a general situation of competition. So instead of talking about The Offensive, it makes more sense to say The Initiative. Second, the equivalent to Mobility for the individual fighter or an army is, in business, Flexibility – the ability to move resources from one application to another. Third, Mass in war finds its business counterpart in Scale. And, finally, in this age of individual autonomy and mobility of employment, Leadership is a more appropriate concept than Command. With these small changes we now have the nine principles of competition to use as a guide and test as we develop business strategies.'

'Wow!' said the new President, his eyes in a bit of a glaze. 'That was an awful lot, awfully quickly. I understood where the principles came from. As a matter of fact that's the *first* time I've understood that. I've heard lots of presentations about principles of business strategy. They've always seemed to me to be just that particular expert's pet theory, which he or she hoped to turn into some consulting dollars! Yours is the first, basic, universal derivation I've ever heard. But I think you need to make each of them a bit clearer if I'm going to be able to use them in practice.'

'OK,' said the Consultant. 'Let's put them into three groups and talk about each in turn.'

'The first group is "The Objective" and "The Initiative," which we combine under the heading Direction. Together they provide everyone in the organization with a clear under-standing of the underlying purpose of every activity, and the core idea on which its strategy is based. This provides a common basis both for planning in advance, and improvisation in action. By adding a short phrase we can also make each principle more easily applicable:

DIRECTION

The Objective: Clear, achievable goals

The Initiative: Quicker and more effective exploitation of emerging trends

'That's much better,' said the new President. 'I can see immediately the practical value of those two. In fact, without them all those concepts of "delegation", "decentralization", and "empowerment" that we're asked to use, are positively dangerous. They'd end up with everyone going off in different directions. What's next?'

'The second group is called "Focus",' said the Consul-tant. 'One of the great military historians, Basil Liddell Hart, once wrote:

> All the lessons of war, not merely one lesson, can be reduced to a single word:
>
> *Concentration*
>
> But, for truth this needs to be amplified to the concentration of strength against weakness.

'The purpose of these three principles is to give us that concentration which, in business, we call focus.

'The three Focus principles are:

FOCUS

Scale: Superior scale in critical resource areas

Economy: Only the necessary resources needed

Flexibility: Ability to move resources around

'Notice that all three of them refer to resources, i.e., people, time and money. From the point of view of planning, that is, deciding what we're actually going to *do* to achieve our objectives, here is the heart of the matter. Without a clear, quantified and focused description of how people, time and money are to be used you don't have a strategy, just an intent.'

'Boy, am I glad to hear you say that,' said the new President. 'I've had all I can take of plans which, when you look closely, are just fancy statements of attractive goals, without any plausible description of the resources that will be needed to achieve them. I think that's one of the most important reasons why people lose faith in their leaders. Raise high expectations, fail to deliver, and you're bound to create cynicism.

'But,' he went on, 'I remember another famous strategic dictum, from Napoleon, who said, "It is impossible to be too strong at the decisive point." How does that square with the principle of Economy?'

'Good question,' said the Consultant. 'This is quite complicated stuff. In fact, in my opinion using it well is *the* distinctive art of the great generals and business strategists. The principle of Scale captures Napoleon's dictum just as it does Hart's. The problem is how to bring about 'superior scale in critical resource areas' in a dynamic world, where competitors are always better at some things than we are. The secret is to remember that everything is relative, and get them to over-allocate in areas we're not interested in. This actually reduces what we need. The idea is to allocate small but sufficient resources (Economy) to stymie our competitors to achieve Napoleon's and Hart's decisive concentration (Scale) in our areas of focus. And because things change, including our competitors' actions, so that we can't know for sure when and where that decisive point will be, we need to be able to move our resources around (Flexibility) to contain any threats and exploit any opportunities. So all three principles play a role in determining how we are to achieve a winning focus.'

'Great,' said the new President. 'What about the other four?'

'The final four principles', said the Consultant, 'are our guide to Implementation, as follows:

IMPLEMENTATION

Unity of Leadership: Shared commitment of key people

Security: Protection from competitive countermoves

Surprise: Amount of unexpected originality involved

Simplicity: Simplicity of the plan

'Those are all pretty self-explanatory,' said the new President.

'Yes,' said the Consultant. 'But don't underestimate their importance. Many is the inferior plan that has been rescued by superb implementation. And, even more important, many is the theoretically brilliant plan that has been wrecked because some key person wasn't on board; or no one had taken into account a major competitor's ability to bring out an equivalent product before the market had switched; or competition was ready with its contingency plans; or the plan was too complicated for anyone to understand.'

'Now, we have turned all this into a simple tool you can use to evaluate strategic options,' finished the Consultant, and handed him another card.

EVALUATING STRATEGIC OPTIONS

	Strategic options		
Principles	**A**	**B**	**C**
Clear, achievable goals			
Exploiting emerging trends			
Superior scale in critical resource areas			
Efficient use of resources			
Flexibility of resources			
Ability to gain commitment			
Protection from competitive countermoves			
Originality and unexpectedness			
Simplicity of the plan			
TOTAL			

Evaluating Questions:

1   What does intuition say about the results?

2   Should any of the principles receive special weighting?

3   Does a very low score anywhere constitute a veto?

'The idea is that you first score each option against each principle. But you don't just add up the numbers and compare the totals to decide which option to choose. Instead you use the results to test your intuition, by asking yourself three evaluating questions.'

1   What does intuition say about the results?

Although, overall, B scored higher than A, I just 'know' that it ought to be the other way around. This will lead you to the second question.

2   Should any of the principles receive special weighting?

Did I come up with the 'wrong' answer because one or more of these principles is particularly important in these circumstances, and my first scoring didn't give it special weighting? Of course you can come up with any answer you like by manipulating the weightings! But if you don't cheat, answering this question will give you a powerful insight as to the crucial variables to look out for (i.e. the ones you need to weight so that the numbers match what you feel deeply is the 'right' answer). However, even then you're not done. You must ask yourself the final question.

3   Does a low score anywhere constitute a veto?

The point is that a disaster can follow from ignoring any of the principles of strategy. There are thirty-eight,

separate questions supporting these rules of thumb –
and the Edsel only failed on two of them! But that was
enough.'

'And your clients all use this thinking?' asked the new President.

'Well, of course they only go through the full exercise for
major decisions, but . . .'

'Yes, I know,' said the new President. 'If you teach
people to think this way, they'll begin applying these ideas as
rules of thumb to every decision that comes up. And, lo and
behold, we've added strategy to operations.'

'You're beginning to catch on,' said the Consultant. And
indeed he was.

The new President returned to his company. He again recorded
what he had learned. He found that he could turn each of the
phrases, which made clear what The Principles of Competition
meant, into a question that he could use as a screen for his plans.
Now he had a simple tool he could use, not just for himself, but
with his people to help them add strategy to operations. As a
first step he began to apply what he'd learned to developing the
purposes and strategies for his company. Once he finished he
had them printed into a beautiful plan. He held a series of
meetings of everyone in the company, gave them the plan and
cleared his desk so it looked like the Grand Strategist's.

STRATEGY: PLAN IT

Success is the reward for excelling at a set of **distinctive capabilities** which have **special** value to a **particular** part of the market-place.

Profitable growth comes from exploiting our strengths, while avoiding our competitors', to satisfy emerging needs.

ACTION PLAN:
FOR STRONGER STRATEGIC POSITIONS

My people know more about their business than I do. I help them not to fail by making sure they take account of the principles of competition:

DIRECTION

1   How clear and achievable are their goals?
2   Are they exploiting emerging trends quickly and effectively?

FOCUS

3   Do they have superior scale in the critical resource areas?
4   Are they using resources efficiently and with minimum waste?
5   Have they built enough flexibility of resources into their plans?

IMPLEMENTATION

6   Does the plan have the ability to gain key people's commitment?

7   How well are they creating barriers to competitive countermoves?

8   How unexpected and original is what they plan to do?

9   How simple are their plans to understand and implement?

PERFORMANCE:

How do
we
deliver
results?

Within a day his desk looked just like it had before. Within a week it was ten times worse. Half of his people weren't implementing his plan at all. And the other half were implementing it in ways contradictory to each other!

He called the Grand Strategist. 'I must have done something wrong,' he said. 'Things are worse than before.'

'No,' said the Grand Strategist. 'I doubt you've done anything wrong. But you may have forgotten to do something right. I have another friend who I think can help.'

This time the new President had to fly to Germany, to visit, of all people, a General on overseas duty. He found this a little odd but the Grand Strategist hadn't failed him yet. The General was bespectacled, charming and not a bit brusque.

'My good friend, the Grand Strategist, tells me you found a bit of a gap between planning and implementation,' he said.

'Yes,' said the new President. 'My people are superb, I know. I'm pretty sure the plan is good. But nothing happened.'

'Your concern then is implementation,' the General stated more than asked. 'I think I know what your problem is, but, if you don't mind, I'd like to ask you a couple of questions to make sure.'

'Who prepared the Plan?'

'Well, I did,' said the new President.

'All by yourself?'

'Yes. Well, no,' said the new President. 'Actually I had some help from an old friend who has quite a good reputation for strategic thinking. He really tested me, and we both felt very good about the final plan.'

'And, at what point did you share the plan with your people, and start on implementing it?' persisted the General.

'We made sure we had all the i's dotted, and t's crossed before we let it see the light of day,' said the new President. 'We wanted to get it just right before anyone saw it. Of course, that cost us a bit of time, but I didn't want my first big effort to have any flaws in it.'

'Three mistakes,' said the General. 'But don't feel bad about it, almost everyone makes them the first time.'

1   The doers must be the planners

'First, and this is not easy for a General to say, people simply don't implement other people's plans any more. Not even in the armed services. That old word 'Command' just doesn't have the power it used to. People want to be involved in creating what they have to execute. Actually that's a very good thing because, with the right guidance, they do it better than we do. If you don't mind me saying so, that is one you should have known. Remember what your job is?'

'Oh, my goodness,' said the new President, looking very crestfallen. 'You're right. My job is to manage the Mission. And here I was getting into the detail of the strategy without involving anyone else. What was my second mistake?'

2   Implementation beats planning

'Well, it too was a pretty natural one,' said the General. 'You wanted to create the perfect plan. And we've learned that there isn't any point to doing that. In fact, the time it takes up in my business, is very dangerous. As one of my predecessors said, "An adequate plan executed now, is much better than a great plan implemented next week." The way I like to put it is that a Grade B plan with Grade A execution always beats a Grade A plan with Grade B execution. Put the effort into getting going, faster and more vigorously. Any mistakes in the plan will be more than made up for by the momentum you establish.'

'That makes sense,' said the new President. 'Actually, I think it fits better with my style than too much of the planning stuff.'

'OK,' said the General. 'But be careful. I didn't say a Grade C, or a Grade D plan. And it's pretty hard to get a B for strategy if your competition is any good. This isn't a recipe for sloppy planning. It just means don't get carried away with all the refinements. A good solid strategy addressing the fundamentals is what you need. Then rapid, vigorous action.'

'What was my third mistake?' asked the new President.

3   Institutionalizing excellence

'That one needs a bit more explaining, and is quite a lot more complicated to put into action,' said the General. 'Have a look at this.' And he handed him a card:

COMBAT EFFECTIVENESS SCORE*

	Western Allies	Germany
Offence		
Winning	1.47	3.02
Losing	1.20	2.28
Defence		
Winning	1.60	2.24
Losing	1.37	2.29

*   'Score' is success at causing casualties, adjusted for the known advantage possessed by the defence.

Source: T.N. Dupuy

'I don't understand,' said the new President. 'What's this got to do with implementing my plan?'

'As I understand it,' said the General, 'you have determined the purposes of your organization and the distinctive capabilities you need to achieve them. And I think, from what you've told me, when you go back and involve them more in your planning you won't have a problem with getting them on board. So what you now need is to help your people learn to excel at executing those capabilities.'

'Yes.'

'This (pointing to the exhibit) is the institutionalization of excellence. Combat Effectiveness measures the ability of an armed force to cause casualties on the other side. That table shows the effectiveness of the Western Allies and the German Armies under the four possible conditions of combat during the Second World War. The ordinary soldier's job is to cause more casualties on the other side than are caused in his. As you can see, the German soldiers outfought their Allied counterparts under all conditions – winning, losing, on offence or defence. That is the most basic, distinctive capability the general seeks to create in his army.

'As Patton said, "No poor, dumb bastard ever won a war by dying for his country. He won it by getting the *other* poor, dumb bastard to die for *his* country." Basically what these numbers boil down to is that four German soldiers could outfight five Western Allied soldiers pretty much as a general rule. That, my friend, is the institutionalization of excellence.'

'Wow,' said the new President. 'If I understood you right, you just said that if we were talking about Basketball, not War, they could have four men out there while we had five and, day in and day out, they'd still beat us, at both ends of the court! That's certainly excellence in my book.'

'Right,' said the General. 'In the Napoleonic Wars the German Army was severely embarrassed by the beating it took. So a small group of its leaders set out to create a system that would institutionalize military excellence and stop it ever happening again. It turns out that what they did was some pretty familiar sounding things. They'll work just as well for you, too.'

'Before you go on,' said the new President, 'there's one thing I think you need to clear up. I suspect you've been asked it before. If the Germans were so good, how come they lost the War?'

'Remember the principles of "The Offensive: Clear, achievable goals," and "Scale: Superior scale in critical resource areas"?' said the General. 'What happens to *achievability* when you decide to take on just about everybody? And, when just one of your opponents has hugely superior scale in *all* resource areas? In your Basketball analogy it would be the same as every time your one team of four beat my team of five, I'd have another team, fresh and ready to go! After a while we'd win, however bad we were.'

'As a matter of fact the American grand strategy has been just that – to throw more resources at a problem than anyone else could afford – from when Lincoln chose Grant to head the Union forces in 1864, to the Vietnamese War, a hundred years later, when an opponent finally came up with a superior idea.

'Of course,' he went on, 'you know what the British grand strategy was during the same period – to *get* the Americans to throw more resources at *their* problems than anyone else could afford!'

The new President laughed. 'I guess that's what Churchill had in mind when on being told about Pearl Harbor he breathed a sigh of relief and said, "Well, after all we won." '

'Exactly,' said the General. 'He had a very clear idea of what had to happen for Britain to win the War.'

'Now, here are the major things the leaders of the German Army concentrated on, starting in the early nineteenth century, that institutionalized excellence.

'Once you have determined your values and purposes and how to achieve them the most powerful tools you have for implementing them are those of people management. It is your people's *behaviour* you must seek to change and that will only happen if the way you select them, evaluate (and reward or punish) them and then train and manage them is clearly and consistently focused on your Mission, and the set of distinctive capabilities you're trying to create. Then . . .

1 Responsibility and the initiative

'As the Grand Strategist told you, your primary control system is your Shared Values. With those in place and with everyone clearly understanding your Purposes you can afford to free people to pursue them as they see the circumstances demand. In other words, you must create a culture of taking personal responsibility, and exercising individual initiative throughout the organization.'

'That doesn't sound very German,' said the new President.

'Not the stereotype we have all been given,' agreed the General. 'In fact there's a wonderful story that T.N. Dupuy, the man who put together those Combat Effectiveness Scores, tells of a German Major being dressed down for some failure in the 1870s by the Crown Prince, then head of the Army. "But, Sir, I was only obeying orders," said the Major in his defence. "Sir," said the Crown Prince, "the Emperor made you a Major because he imagined you would know when to disobey his orders!"'

2 Attention to relevant detail

'Ah, I know this one,' said the new President. 'You mean getting things right the first time. Avoiding sloppiness. But not nitpicking.'

'Yes,' said the General, 'but there's a bit more to it than

"not nitpicking". It is a real art telling the relevant details, which must be got dead right, from the ones which can safely be left as "good enough". My son's teacher is forever telling him that "history is in the details". But that, by itself, is not enough. Discernment is the key. Knowing which detail contains the vital insight is the mark of the great historian or, in my profession, fine intelligence analyst. And a manager, trying to decide what to make of a mass of data or a complicated plan, has to have that skill too.

'The discerning manager can save his or her people a huge amount of effort by guiding them towards the things that really make a difference. And *that's* where it's impossible to put too much effort on getting the details right.'

'Discerning the key information, using it to get your people to focus on the most important things and *then* making sure the details are just right,' said the new President. 'I can certainly see how that leads to superior implementation. What's next?'

3   Objectivity, and the study of experience

'Learning from our mistakes and not rationalizing failures,' the new President interjected again. 'I'm beginning to get the sense of a rather unusual kind of elite outfit as we go through these.

'But in my experience,' he went on, 'the more successful a group is, and the longer its success is sustained – which are the roots of eliteness, I think – the more pride is likely to get in the way of objectivity, and rationalization in the way of examining the reasons for things going wrong.'

'You're absolutely right,' said the General. 'It's very difficult to maintain the humility necessary to learn from one's mistakes, when success keeps piling on success. Nevertheless, throughout the hundred-odd years of its European pre-eminence the German Army was the *only* army in the world with a department dedicated to the study of history, including its own mistakes! To be sure, it had at least its share of overbearing autocrats but, underneath, there was a system dedicated to what, today, I think we'd call continuous improvement.'

4   Pervasive application

'No compromises, right?' said the new President.

'Yes,' said the General. 'My wife's Bridge teacher once told her that everything in bridge is 95 per cent, meaning you have to know when to break the rules. That's a great guide to the use of day-to-day, operational rules. But it's no good for the fundamental principles on which an organization is founded. The great companies, indeed great organizations of all kinds, are prepared to go to apparently absurd lengths to stay true to their principles. It's the price they pay for real excellence. But the pay-off is for ever, in superior performance.'

'Let me check I understand all this,' said the new President. 'First I set my Mission, and determine the distinctive capabilities I want to develop. Then I put the bulk of my effort into institutionalizing them into the way I manage my people. And I rely on my people to find the right ways to implement the plan. That's a completely different kind of organization from the ones most of us are used to. But I can sure understand how powerful it must be when it works. Now I'm beginning to see what the Grand Strategist means when he says he doesn't run the business. He doesn't need to – as long as he manages the Mission.'

The new President fell silent. The awesome potential of this new way of thinking was getting through to him. He thanked the General for his help and left to catch his plane home. On the way back he added to his growing game plan.

IMPLEMENTATION: DO IT

Organizations do not take action, people do. And people only implement what they are involved in creating.

Grade A execution of a Grade B plan always beats Grade B execution of a Grade A plan.

ACTION PLAN:
FOR HIGHER QUALITY IMPLEMENTATION

Selection, evaluation and training, and the way I manage my people are my most powerful tools for fulfilling our mission. I will:

☐   inculcate and reward personal responsibility and individual initiative in every one of my people

☐   pay close attention to detail where it matters to my strategy, and not pick my people's plans to pieces when it doesn't

☐   learn from our mistakes and be objective in my evaluation of our experience

☐   allow no exceptions to our mission, and go to any lengths to be true to it

As he wrote it, a nagging worry kept coming into the back of his mind. So as soon as he was home, he called the General.

CHANGE:
How do we
cope with
change?

1 NOTHING FAILS LIKE SUCCESS

'What's the problem?' asked the General.

'Well,' said the new President, 'I was remembering the second division I was given to run. When I first joined it, in many ways it resembled the kind of organization we were talking about – everyone had a clear idea of its mission, though they didn't call it that; people shared the same set of beliefs about what should guide the way they acted, and the *esprit de corps* was incredible. Then over the space of a very small number of years it fell apart. I was put in to pick up the pieces but it was too late to salvage much. Doesn't that rather damage the theory?'

'If I understand you,' said the General, 'the division went on behaving as it always had, but it no longer worked the way it always had?'

'That's right,' said the President.

'Did you find out why?'

'Yes, we did. As a matter of fact we hired a very expensive consultant who documented the disaster in great depth. Unfortunately he wasn't quite as good at suggesting how we got out of the mess, as at explaining how we'd got into it. Boiling it down to its essence, the market no longer needed what we were providing and a new set of competitors without our overheads undercut us to hell.'

'Did your customers no longer like the way your people behaved?'

'Oh no, that wasn't the problem. They still felt we were by far the best people to deal with. They just didn't want to pay for the kind of product and service we were selling. As a matter of fact they were quite right. They didn't need to. The business had changed. But by the time we were prepared to accept that it was too late. Whenever I think of it I get mad. We were the recognized leaders, we had the finest people and there wasn't anything our competitors did that we couldn't have done better and earlier. What made it worse, I discovered our own people saw it coming but couldn't get management to listen. Talk about a failure of leadership.'

'I think you've answered your own question,' said the General. 'It takes us back to Thomas Watson. Remember: "If an organization is to meet the challenge of a changing world, it must be prepared to change everything about itself except its beliefs." But it has to be said that this is the most challenging of all the tasks you will face. We call it the task of Renewal. The Grand Strategist suggested someone for you to talk to about it if you like.'

*

A couple of weeks later the new President visited his next and, as it turned out, final mentor. She was President of a company located about a hundred miles from his own office, so he drove himself over one grey, November morning. He found himself driving through a grimy industrial town which could have served as a model of the rust belt. In fact, he assumed, the whole area was a memorial to the kind of management and inflexibility that had caused the disaster in the division he had discussed with the General.

The factory was much the same from the outside as many he'd driven past: red brick, grimy with soot and belching steam from its chimneys. But even before he reached the reception he could tell something was different. First, the security guard on the gate had been very friendly. He not only expected the new President, but knew why he was there!

'Come to learn the Good Fairy's magic, then?' he was greeted. 'Hope you have as much fun while you're here as we do every day.'

Unusual. To say the least.

When he got inside it was just the same. There was a notice welcoming him, and on the receptionist's desk there was a sign which said, 'Vice-President on deck'.

Vice-President? On deck?

'Hi,' the man behind the sign said cheerfully. 'I'm Chris, the Chief Bean Counter around here. It's my day on deck.'

'Your day on deck?'

'Yes. We don't have a receptionist here. The Vice-Presidents take turns at it. And we also man those two phones. The red one is for anyone in the company who has something to complain about. The green one is for anyone with an idea on how to improve something. The numbers are 999 and 111, so they're easy for everyone to remember.'

Just then the door to the reception area opened and a woman about the same age as the new President came through.

'Hi,' she said, 'I'm Kathy. Glad to see you. Sorry I wasn't here to greet you. They'd hidden my telephone. I'll have to suggest they think up another punishment.'

'Punishment?'

'Yes. I insisted on a lower price for a recent bid than my people said was needed to win. They were right. So they punished me by hiding my telephone. Actually they've also hidden my chairs, too. But we'll fool them; we'll use the Boardroom.'

The Boardroom was – well, it was different. For a start there was no table. Then there were the chairs. A group of very comfy-looking leather armchairs were clustered together. Next to them was a collection of nine chairs of random shapes and sizes, each with a name on it – The Good Fairy; Chief Bean Counter; The Magician; The Lean, Mean, Manufacturing Machine; General Terry; People Person; Monsieur Le Marketing; Desperate Dan; and Media Mogul.

'What on earth . . .' began the new President.

'They're my management team,' said his hostess. 'Like their titles? The other chairs are for the Board members; we like to keep them as comfy as possible.'

The new President looked around. The decorations were as weird as the chairs. They reminded him of . . . could it be? Yes, definitely, a funfair!

'This is your boardroom?' he finally exploded. 'Don't you do anything serious around here?'

'Well, we make more money than anyone else in our industry,' said his hostess. 'Oh yes, and we're outgrowing everyone too if that's what you mean. And we set goals, review our progress, hire and fire people, and praise and reprimand each other. Yes, I guess we do a lot of serious things around here. But we try not to do any of them seriously.'

'I think you'll have to explain,' said her guest.

'OK,' she said. 'I think you're here to explore how we tackle the task of renewal. That is, how we avoid the problem of getting stuck in our ways, however good they are, so that we don't get caught by changes in the environment?'

The new President nodded.

2 DON'T RESEARCH – EXPERIMENT

The best summary of the change problem that I've ever seen is this,' said his hostess, handing him a card.

MTBD > MTBS

'A very observant lady, Rosabeth Moss Kanter, wrote that in a book called *The Changemasters*. What it says is:

> The Mean Time Between Decisions is greater than
> the Mean Time Between Surprises!

'In other words, in most organizations it takes them longer to make a decision than it does for the assumptions on which the decision is based to change in some way they had not foreseen!'

The new President laughed. 'Boy, is that the truth,' he said.

'And it's not just in the giant bureaucracies that it's happening,' said his hostess. 'It's catching up with all of us because of the accelerating change we're all experiencing.'

'So, the solution has to be a drastic shortening of the

time from seeing the need to implementing the innovation,' said the new President.

'Well, we think you have to go even further than that,' his companion said. 'We think that the process has to start before you see the need if you really want to make sure you get there first.'

'But that means random experimentation,' protested her visitor. 'Surely that can't be economic.'

'Oh no, it's not random,' she replied. 'Our people know our business very well and they instinctively rule out the really silly ideas. But it does mean a lot of failures. Considerably more than half of what we try, as a matter of fact. However, a 0.333 average will get you pretty close to the Baseball batting title most years. It's the same with innovation. It doesn't take many successes to pay for a lot of failures, particularly if you catch them early enough. And, you know, those failures often aren't anywhere as bad as they seem. Let me give you an example.

'I have a good friend who makes his living teaching managers about strategy. When he started no one knew him, and the firm he worked with didn't do a very good job in marketing his workshops. The worst moment came when, just two weeks before what he had planned to be a major event in Chicago, only two people had signed up. Of course he had to cancel it and send those two their money back. He was acutely embarrassed, and worried that this failure would really hurt his career. Then one of his colleagues, trying to comfort him, pointed out that other than themselves, there were only two people in the whole world who knew of the failure! Ever since he hasn't been afraid of trying just about anything. That's what we try to do here, too.'

'Well, your success certainly speaks for itself,' said the new President. 'But that doesn't explain why this place resembles a funfair as much as a factory.'

'Two reasons,' said his hostess. 'First, do you see that sign over there?'

The new President looked where she was pointing – a small poster on the wall, on which was written:

ALL THE HORSES JUMP

NO CHIPPED PAINT

WINDOWS DON'T GET DIRTY

NO STALE POPCORN

'Do you know what that is?' and, when her guest shook his head, she went on, 'it's the design specifications for Disney-world in California. Walt Disney visited a rather rundown amusement park with one of his children. When he came back he said, "it's got to be possible to create a park where all the horses jump, there's no chipped paint, windows don't get dirty and there's no stale popcorn". This room, and that sign, remind us that it's the simple stuff, done right, that is often the biggest innovation of all.'

'I buy into that immediately,' said the new President,

'it's extraordinary the advantage one can get over one's competitors by doing the little things customers appreciate. It's not just the basic product people want, but the whole package of things that go with it. I like nothing better than products that the so-called experts have started to refer to as "commodities". It usually means there's a great opportunity to differentiate yourself through superb service, which everybody else has forgotten about. What's the second reason?'

3 FOSTERING INNOVATION

'Remember what the Grand Strategist told you about Shared Values being the only control system that doesn't rely on fear?' Kathy asked the new President. 'And that one of the reasons that was important was to help create a climate for creativity and innovation?'

'Yes,' said the new President.

'Well, what we've found is that the more fun people have, the more creative they are, the more things they try out and so the more successful innovation we get around here. Making sure there's a spirit of play about everything we do is the best weapon I have for ensuring we never stop questioning whether we can do things better, and encouraging people to try out even the craziest of ideas. It just works.'

'Mind you,' she went on, 'it's pretty hard work making sure everyone has fun. And you'd be surprised at the discipline it requires of my leadership team.'

'What do you mean?' asked the new President.

'You can't just make a declaration and send out a memo saying "from now on we'll have fun around here",' said his hostess. 'Sadly most people have been taught to expect the opposite. They think work is supposed to be serious stuff, and confuse the importance of the result with the way to behave to get it. If you let him, the Grinch won't just steal Christmas, he'll steal the fun right out of your day. So we have to work hard to stop him. It's not what we say that creates the culture around here; it's what we do. How I and my management team spend its time; what we reward . . . and punish; whom we promote; and, where we spend our money. These are the things that determine the real climate of our organization. And, boy, is it difficult to make sure we're always consistent, in all those activities, with the message we want everyone to receive.'

'So that's why you have Vice-Presidents on deck,' said the new President. 'And a funfair for a Boardroom. And let your people punish you for your mistakes.'

'Right,' said Kathy. 'And have a hot line for good ideas, and another for things people are unhappy about. And, and, and, and . . .'

'Are there any other secrets I should know?' asked the new President.

'Well, they're hardly secrets,' laughed his hostess. 'But, yes, there are three other things that are important to prevent success turning into failure because of an inability to change.

'The first is to develop in everyone the ability to work in groups. Innovation is all about teams and trust, and improvisation and learning from each other. My son is a very keen tennis player and that's great because it teaches him discipline and personal responsibility – there's no one else he can blame for what happens. But I'm glad he plays soccer, too. Learning teamwork, experiencing the joy of winning as a team, these are things we all need if we're going to keep our organizations healthy over the long haul. And it's never too early to start.

'Second, the way we react to bad news, or criticism is a sure sign of whether we're serious about maintaining an open, fun-filled organization. And, of course, the further we go in our careers, the more our egos get flattered, and so the more difficult it becomes. Once a leader leaves the impression that he or she can't take bad news, it's the end of candour and truth as a way of life. I can't emphasize enough how difficult it is, and how important it is to maintain a climate of openness.

'Third, and very closely connected to what I've just described, we have to help people enjoy arguing, and do it constructively. There is a tremendous tendency in organizations, and it gets worse the more successful they are, to want to banish discord and forbid conflict. That's not only not the real world, it kills questioning, testing and eventually even the refining of ideas that come up. It turns the organization into a binary world. Everything has to be voted up or down, things can only be good or bad, you can only be for them or against them. When you think that, unless you have a genius to rely on, all ideas are at first bad ideas; unless we learn the good in them and work on it most of them are going to die. After all most babies are pretty ugly, aren't they? Except to their mothers, of course! And so it is with ideas. So we have to learn to argue, and enjoy it – and if the boss doesn't, no one else will. Mind you if the boss always wins, it's over too. As I said, it's tough.'

All through this the new President was scribbling notes furiously. When his hostess had finished he showed her what he'd written to see if he'd got it right.

RENEWAL: CHANGE IT

Experimentation is the best way to find and test new ideas.

I cannot dictate that there will be innovation. I can only create a climate that fosters it.

ACTION PLAN:
FOR MORE EFFECTIVE RENEWAL

How to spend my time, what I reward . . . and punish, whom I promote and where I allocate our resources will determine the real climate of my organization. I will:

- ☐   conduct all our affairs in a spirit of play and make sure it is possible for everyone else to do the same

- ☐   model and reinforce the ability to work in groups

- ☐   encourage constructive argument and help my people enjoy it

- ☐   remain open to criticism and never shoot the bearers of bad news

'That's it,' she said. 'Looks pretty simple written down, doesn't it? But it's a full-time job making it happen.'

'Thank you so much for your time,' said the new President. 'I hope I may come back when I get stuck. I think I'm going to need to.'

'Of course you can; we'll be delighted to see you,' said his hostess, as she walked him back to the reception area.

'Maybe you'd like to send some of your people, too. We're always happy to tell our story and hear other people's experiences. That's a better way of learning than always having to make your own mistakes.

'As a matter of fact—' pointing to some of the offices they were walking past '—we have some pretty good experts in their own fields whom some of your Vice-Presidents might like to meet. There's Dick – he runs our Lean, Mean, Manufacturing Machine. Even the Grand Strategist consults him on manufacturing matters. Then there's Bob – Monsieur Le Marketing, French background you see – he's probably the most innovative person we've got; and Desperate Dan, he runs International.'

'Desperate Dan?' queried the new President.

'Yes,' she said. 'Actually, he's not so desperate now. But he used to work for a guy who couldn't make a decision. Believe me, that'll make you desperate in a hurry.'

'I notice the "People Person's" office – I guess that's your personnel guy – is empty,' said the new President. 'Don't you have one?'

'Not at the moment,' said the hostess. 'When we began to change everything around here, we tried one of the managers who'd grown up here because he knew the place. That was my mistake. Great guy. But he just wasn't able to make the transition. And appointing him simply wasn't consistent with the message. So we're going outside. We've found a super guy, a Scotsman, actually; he starts next week.'

'What about R&D?' asked the new President.

'That's Jim, The Magician. Give him some earth, air, fire and water, and before you know where you are, he's conjured up a new product. He's in his own building. And, yes, we've got some really interesting ideas about managing product development we'd love to share,' continued his hostess. 'I'd also like you to meet our Media Mogul, Robin. An awful lot of this new way of managing has to do with Communications.'

By this time they were back at the entry to the building. Chris, 'the receptionist', stood up to say goodbye to the new President.

'I expect you'd like one of these,' he said, handing him a plastic card. The new President looked at it and, almost in shock, stuttered, 'But it's got everything I've learned from everyone from The Grand Strategist onward written on it.'

'Right,' said the Chief Bean Counter and his boss almost in unison. 'You see we've all travelled the same path. President, bean counters, the R&D folks, manufacturing, everyone. So it's not very surprising that we've all learned the same lessons. In fact, one of the lessons is that *everyone* has a part to play in this new way of managing. Grand Strategy is a discipline for everyone on the team, all of the time.'

'May I have some more for my people?' asked the new President.

'Sure,' said the hostess. 'But you'll need to think very carefully about how you use them. Remember what happened to your first big plan.'

'I will,' said the new President. 'No more trying to do things by myself. I'll need to help them learn this for themselves. I'll probably need someone who's done this before to help me.'

'We did,' said Kathy. 'Try the Consultant the Grand Strategist sent you to. He's different. He helped us a lot.'

'Well, goodbye, and thank you so much,' said the new President. 'I never expected this journey would end up in a funfair! I can't wait to build my, sorry, our own.'

'Goodbye,' said the hostess. 'And welcome to the club. There aren't many of us yet. But you'd be surprised how fast we're growing.'

CONCLUSION:

THE WINNING ORGANIZATION

The new President spent some time digesting what he'd learned; looking at each of the pieces, relating each to each other and reflecting on how they all worked together as a whole. He was pretty sure he was going to be able to apply it. Obviously he was going to make mistakes, maybe even some big ones, but that was OK. As he'd learned, it went with the territory. It was part of the learning and growing process.

He decided it was time to say thank you, so he called the Grand Strategist one last time.

'Come on over,' said the Grand Strategist when he picked up the phone. 'I've got a couple more things I'd like to share with you to wrap things up.'

So, a few days later, only a few months after his first rather nervous visit, the new President found himself again in the Grand Strategist's office looking at that bare desk, with the pad, and the pencil, and the plaque that he still couldn't read but, he now knew, said:

If I manage our Mission I can rely on everyone else to run the business.

Before I take any action I ask myself:

'In what way will this action embody our Values?'

'In what way will this action contribute to our Purposes?'

1 LEADERSHIP

'I'm sure you have realized', began the Grand Strategist when they were both seated, 'that what you've been learning doesn't have a lot in common with "management" as we've all been taught it. And it's not just something that only Chairmen or Presidents can do.'

'Yes,' said the new President. 'This is a whole new way of thinking about *every* position in the organization, because there's a bit of Grand Strategy in everyone's job. In fact it seems to me the word "management" itself doesn't really apply to it at all. I think this is really "leadership" isn't it?'

'You're right, and it can't be emphasized enough,' said the Grand Strategist. 'What you've been learning is a system which can help you, and all of your managers, first lead a winning organization, of *any* kind and any *size*; and second, play your part in keeping it healthy so that it goes on winning from one generation to another.'

'But what you've learned can't do it for you by itself. It is terribly important to remember that the system is just a tool, albeit a very powerful one, for leadership; leadership is not a component of the system. What you do with it is very much in your hands.

'You've heard the Roman Catholic Church, IBM and the German Army used as examples of this system in action. All of them at times have suffered enormous failures of leadership, which have caused them to do much harm to themselves and to others. Simply by adopting the *processes* that make up the system doesn't absolve you from the responsibility for the *content* you put into it. The choices you make – above all of goals to pursue, of strategies to fund, and of people to employ – as well as the way you manage, will determine the success you and your organization will enjoy.

'Having made those choices, you'll find your role, as leader, is more to coach than to control, more to remove obstacles than to pass judgements and, most of all, more to manage the way your organization is managed, than to try to run the detail of the business. The same thinking applies to *anyone* with *any* kind of department to run or, for that matter, team to coach or group to lead. Whenever there are obstacles to overcome, other people involved in implementation and things are liable to change unexpectedly, these ideas are the secret of success.

'Most of us are still pretty uncomfortable with all these new roles at first. We've been proud of how reliable, how in control we have been seen to be. We've regarded ourselves as having very good judgement and have come to enjoy making snappy decisions. And we've been raised to be hands-on, take-charge kinds of people. We have to let most of that go when we're put in charge of other people. But we have to retain our toughness, and learn to apply it in a different way – in our determination to help people be the best they can be, in the rigour we insist on in the development of strategy, and in the consistency with which we use our Values and our Purposes as the final test of what we and our organizations do.'

'Although I don't yet know how to do it all, I now know just what you mean,' said the new President. 'I think it's the most exciting thing I've ever been confronted with. Already I am seeing dramatic changes in my people and our results. It's simply extraordinary what they can do as I learn how to lead them properly. Our competition doesn't know what hit them.

'You have no idea how grateful I am to you, to the Consultant you sent me to see, to the General and to Kathy – the Good Fairy,' he finished, with a chuckle.

'Yes, I have,' said the Grand Strategist. 'Remember, you're not the first. I've been down the road, too. Everybody has to. You can't get there without travelling the same path. But you should thank yourself too. You recognized your need. You made the start. And you stayed the course. I'm looking forward to seeing what you make of it. I hope you'll keep in touch. It'll be my turn to learn from you next.'

'I do have one, last question, if you don't mind,' said the new President.

'Fire away,' said the Grand Strategist.

'Why do they call you . . .' he began.

'. . . the Grand Strategist?' finished his host. 'There are two ways of answering – one rather, well, "grand", and the other quite practical and as a matter of fact, a good summary of what you've been learning. Let's start with the grand one.

'History shows, very broadly speaking, that the nations of the world have gone through alternating periods of conflict between each other which are best described as Limited War and Total War. It makes a lot of sense that this should be so. A period of total war so exhausts and horrifies people that they resolve never to let it happen again. Governments, responding to this demand, voluntarily restrict themselves to more limited war. Then, as memories fade, and small causes accumulate into big ones, the passage of time, and often some great cataclysmic event will reinitiate a period of total war until the devastation it causes finally produces another "never again" resolution.

'We have been in a period of limited war since the end of the Second World War. The preceding period of total war began with the French Revolution in 1789. With that event the Napoleonic armies changed war from a limited, stylized duel between armies, governed by strict conventions, into a struggle between nations with all of the national resources thrown into the fray. Armies fighting armies is what Strategy is all about. Nations fighting nations is what Grand Strategy is about.'

'So, putting that in business language, it's because of the

much greater competitive intensity that we face today, and therefore the involvement of all of a company's resources all the time, that we need a bigger concept than Strategy?' asked the new President, to check that he'd understood.

'That's right,' said the Grand Strategist. 'But there's also the other, more down-to-earth explanation which you may prefer. I'd like to stay with the military analogy to explain it.

'Think of two armies marching across a plain,' he went on. 'On the other side of the plain there is a hill. Strategy says we to get on the hill because that's the *stronger strategic position*. However, we could still lose an ensuing battle if the other guy outfights us. So Grand Strategy has also to be concerned with ensuring *higher quality implementation*. Now, the problem we face in business, that those two armies don't face, is that the hill may move! Remember MTBD>MTBS. This isn't just a question of a change in tactics. The *hill* moved! The very basis of our strategy. We have to be able to change even our most basic plans in midstream, or I guess I should have said, mid-march, to take account of the unexpected. And do it better, and quicker than the other guy. In other words, in business terms, Grand Strategy must also ensure *more effective renewal* of our plans as the world changes, and of our organizations themselves from one generation to the next, than our competitors.'

'So Grand Strategy simply encompasses the three sets of rules and actions that you learned from the Consultant, the

General, and the Good Fairy. Plus, don't forget, what you and I talked about – the *shared values* and *shared purposes* that make up our mission. Without those we don't know why we're doing all the other things, that is why we even exist as an organization, and what it is we're trying to "win" at.

'It's not really a very intimidating idea, though I must admit some of my colleagues have turned it into a rather intimidating name.'

2 THE NEW GRAND STRATEGIST

The new President worked hard to put what he'd learned into practice. His company prospered and grew. It became one of 'the' places to look for a job. And it wasn't very long before he received a rather surprising phone call. The person on the other end of the line sounded desperate, and not a little nervous.

'Is that the, um, Grand Strategist?' she asked.

'Who?' he said.

'Maybe I've got the wrong number,' she said.

Then it struck him. With a big grin he said, 'No, you've got the right number; what can I do to help?'

And before long he was helping another person along the road to becoming, herself, a Grand Strategist.

3 YOU CAN BE ONE TOO

All it takes is to want to, enough.

THE GRAND STRATEGIST'S CREDO

MISSION: DETERMINE IT

Shared Values provide **CONTROL** by guiding behaviour

Shared Purposes provide **FOCUS** by driving strategy

If I manage our Mission I can rely on everyone else to run the business

Before I take any decision I ask myself:

'In what way will this action embody our Values?'
'In what way will this action contribute to our Purposes?'

STRATEGY: PLAN IT

Success is the reward for excelling at a set of distinctive capabilities that have special value to a particular part of the market-place

Profitable growth comes from exploiting our strengths, while avoiding our competitors', to satisfy emerging needs

RENEWAL: CHANGE IT

Experimentation is the best way to find and test new ideas

I cannot dictate that there will be innovation. I can only create a climate that fosters it

IMPLEMENTATION: DO IT

Organizations do not take action, people do. And people only implement what they are involved in creating

Grade A execution of a Grade B plan always beats Grade B execution of a Grade A plan